THE MARTIAN'S REGRESS

THE MARTIAN'S REGRESS

REGRESS

J. O. Morgan

CAPE POETRY

1 3 5 7 9 10 8 6 4 2

Jonathan Cape, an imprint of Vintage,
20 Vauxhall Bridge Road,
London SW1V 2SA

Jonathan Cape is part of the Penguin Random House
group of companies whose addresses can be found
at global.penguinrandomhouse.com

Penguin
Random House
UK

Published by Jonathan Cape in 2020

penguin.co.uk/vintage

A CIP catalogue record for this book
is available from the British Library

ISBN 9781787332140

Typeset by the author
Printed and bound in Great Britain
by TJ International Ltd, Padstow, Cornwall

Penguin Random House is committed to a sustainable future
for our business, our readers and our planet. This book is made
from Forest Stewardship Council® certified paper.

MIX
Paper from
responsible sources
FSC
www.fsc.org
FSC® C018179

to
a companionable soul

CONTENTS

THE MARTIAN'S REGRESS

A Dream of Planetary Subjugation

They found her drifting
Sleepy-headed
Barely a breath left in her
Barely anything at all
As scant in body as in brain
Content in her unrivalled emptiness

She was easy, docile, didn't notice
When they probed her
When their roving fingers found
Her weak spots
Fed their straws in
Very deep to touch upon her cooled-hard heart

And the shock
As she was jumpstarted back
Into hot-blooded wakefulness
It wasn't enough to throw their hooks
They'd expected a struggle and
She writhed right into their hands

Even as she drew herself more tightly into herself
They sought to shush her
Blew their smoky rings around her
Trapping her under a laminar flow
That lensed the light
And burned her pink skins bright

They offered her water, she sipped
They tipped the cup, she spluttered, gagged
They jammed the bronze head of their hose
Between her teeth
And eased the pressure up
Forcing her to swallow every drop

And when at last she cried out, gurgling
So they scattered liberally their seed
Amid her softnesses
And left her in a fevered foam of sweat
Her breathing hot, her hollows threaded
Rough with roots

The Martian Struggles Alone

Waking from his nightmare in the rocket
Was like waking from a nightmare anywhere else
The pressing blackness of the air
Failed to hide the martian from himself.
The nightmare too had woken.

He fumbled for his bedside lamp
Sought comfort in its feeble yellow glow.
But the capsule of his room was wallpapered
Patterned in homely tangles of thick green vines
With broad black faces leering through the gaps.

The martian tore the paper off in strips.
But the metal beneath was embossed
With an identical design.
He struck at it with a lump hammer but
The faces, freshly mangled, still grinned out.

He shut his eyes
Feeling his way to the bathroom,
One sharp glimpse of himself in the mirror
And he turned both taps full on.

The mirror misted.
Still his squat black shadow was there
Lurking behind the fog.

He shattered the glass
His image multiplied
Each facet conforming to a dark homogeneity.
The nightmare had discovered new strength in numbers.

The martian bundled the torn wallpaper and fragments of mirror
Into the airlock
Zeroed the pressure and opened the outer hatch.

The pieces floated just outside
Keeping pace with the rocket,
The paper slowly flexing
A permanent wave
While the mirrors turned and flashed.

The martian consulted his wardrobe for further solutions.

His spacesuit had been made to mimic his skin,
It accentuated his pot-belly bulge
It scaffolded snugly his charcoal-stick limbs
The inner curve of its bubble helmet
Casting back a weak wide-eyed reflection
Whichever way he looked.

He had a mind to rend holes in the fabric
But thought better of it.
At least it wasn't quite as black as him.

Outside he kicked at the debris and each piece
Wobbled slowly guiltily away.
It brought him a little relief.

He turned to face the rocket,
The stillness of its silhouette
Centring a hollow sphere of stars
And every black inch of its long narrow length
Recalling the source of his nightmare.

He unclipped himself from his tether
And drifted

                     But only for a moment.
The full lonely weight of himself in that moment
Becoming the only weight.

Perhaps if he searched the rocket
Thoroughly
He might just discover some trivial recreation, some modest
   distraction.

He reapplied the clip
And took his chance.

Ancestral Tales

The first among martians was weak, inefficient
Tall and leafy, near-translucent
He wilted under the sapping waves of the sun.
His sweat steamed, the steam smoked, he toiled
To tame a land that would not yield
Leastways not to him. So lightweight he
Could barely hold his feet upon the ground.
He reddened and blistered, he withered and crumbled
At last giving all of himself, becoming soil.

The second martian was an angry man.
Confident in his broad-built self, with a firm belief
In thick protective lotions, he punished the land. The land
Gave meekly back. It sucked in everything he plied it with.
And still the fine pink dot of the sun
Pressed hard against his spine. He bore the weight
For a while. But all that while it hammered him
Bit by bit into the anvil earth. He never gave up.
Till as a bitter seed he planted himself.

The third martian was small and fat. Very heavy.
And being born black all over he met the sun
As no more than a neighbour, as inferior, its heat rays
Passing straight through that blackness unchanged and so
He always felt too cold. But he never grumbled.
His dark insides like hardwood made him patient.
He chewed things over slowly needing little sustenance.
No care for much beyond himself, nor even for himself,
He continued impervious—never again to be subdued.

As a boy his crime was sneakery, a determined pickpocket.
As a girl her crime was argument, a fierce contrary nature.

His punishment was exposure on the high plateau where
  the stacked skies were at their thinnest.
Hers was to be lowered headfirst into a deep and oily pool.

Unfiltered, the bared sun roasted him to a sooty blackness.
She bubbled in the lightless depths, she breathed those treacles in.

And the sun seared the tethers from his wrists.
And the oils soaped the rope from her feet.

A shadow descending in patient fury they never knew it till
  he was upon them.
Flopping from the pool with her new inky sheen she slipped
  right through their groping fingers.

———

And when these two at length found each other
Their numerous progeny, greasy, small
And black inside and out
Roamed the land through the silent night
Seizing those to whom they took a fancy
Men and women and children alike,
Spreading further their blackness
Infusing the whole populace
Setting a tough precedent
Strengthening a race.

An Adaptable Song

And there were those that lingered by the swamps, in the shade
Of the tall mallow trees. And if they learned to hide to breathe
In green mud-clotted pools, still, they couldn't stay under forever
Each was soon harpooned and dragged to land.
  (We were young, we were naked and hungry, we dug
  Our bolt-holes deep into the riverbank.
  We curled up inside peering out.)

And of those with the widest throats, who moaned at moons
Who pounded their chests, exerting their authority,
They made too much of a racket to notice us creeping up behind.
  (There was strength in the length of our fingers.
  With slippered feet we stalked through unlocked doors,
  Extending the blessed silences of sleep.)

Even those with long legs who escaped into
The hot grey mountain heights, they were too wiry
Too insubstantial, we needed only to loiter nearby
Till they sank inwardly, till they wavered and fell
Leaving their soft slender bones for us to gather.
  (Stout-limbed, hump-backed, we prided ourselves
  On internal stock-keeping, a subdermal larder of fats.
  Our minds kept small and safe behind thick walls.)

But of those with big ears and black eyes who had a sense
When we were about. And of those with tougher skins who bore
The constant needling of the distant sun. And of those
Who snuck up close and robbed the sweetbreads from our bowls.
We welcomed them all as our siblings, yes, as equals into the fold.
  (We made our own laws and we stuck to them.
  We had purpose, we took necessary measures—
  Understanding what was needed to endure.)

The Martian Unpacks His Companion

Her soft rubber skin had been left a pure bright white.
Adding dye only weakened the mixture
Splitting when it set.

White showed up any scuffs and abrasions.
She was made to be non-marking
Her body was wipeably clean.

That doubled height
Those gangly limbs
The overt femininities

All relics of an ancient era.
Hers was the only moulding they'd found intact
                         though the wiring was new.

A womanly shell with the woman removed
Refilled with simple logic gates
Bloodless thoughtless yet obedient.

As insects are content to possess a pared-down intellect
She was content.

Nine-tenths of her processing power was used up
Directing the fluid motion of her limbs,
With pressures exerted through each fingertip
Neither over-tightening nor ever letting slip,
And rapid adjustments of balance in silently
Shifting herself from his path.

The essence of her design was in not being noticed
Till she was required to be noticed
Of blending unobtrusively with other furniture.

Her perfectly still face
Her slightly parted lips
Forever on the cusp of enlightened pronouncement
Though never a word not a peep was uttered through them.
Words were his preserve not hers,
Appropriate action the only response
Her soft eager stare indicative of her alertness.

Unwavering devotion was her primary directive.
He might strike her in a moment of frustration
She'd cling to the short-lived memory of his touch,
He might issue his wearisome instructions
For the umpteenth time
She'd find fresh nuance in his tone
She'd savour its every buzz,
He could shun her ignore her dismiss her
She'd follow meekly at his heel.

And if he commanded her to stay
She'd study him keenly
As he walked away
And in his absence
Would strain every sensor
Her pistons and gauges and coils in mute readiness
Waiting for that follow-up command.

The Natural Course of Things

And if the sun had begun to burn itself ever brighter
We widened the hole, we let its new dazzle in

And if the air had already started turning foul
We did all we could to quicken what was unavoidable

And if the cattle lay moaning in their death throes
We'd bred more than we needed anyhow

And if the birds floundered and came down to earth with a thump
We had our own superior flying machines

We flew further and faster and all on a single tank
We cut the sky to ribbons in our race

And as the fish slowly rotted alive in their ponds
We added a powerful detergent to clean up the water

We had the filters running day and night
Everything was pure by the time it got through to us

All this had been foreseen, such cycles are predictable
And we took the impetus, we rushed up to meet it

The planet may have been going downhill
But we were forging ahead, we were leading the way

We might have stayed on for several millennia more
But there's much to be said for a change of scenery

Martian Toasting Ritual

On a low wooden table lacquered in silver and black
He places his implements
An oil burner, tongs, a dish for catching crumbs,
A fine stiff blade.

He trims the wick ensuring the flame
Will burn with a steady point.

The bread has been readied pre-trip, his own hands
Shaping each oblong of dough, slow-baked
And packed in plywood crates to bring aboard.

Small white rectangular loaves,
The length of his soft black palm
The width of his slender wrist,
Each loaf individually wrapped in yellow muslin.

He shaves off a heel and discards it
Cuts again, and again discards, and so on
Till he is certain, knowing by sight
The bared end is perfectly square.

Each wafer curled off with a single smooth sweep of the knife.

The first perfect slice is likewise discarded.
Perfection should not be attained through accident—
He aims for consistency, for a sense
Of sustainability.

Eight identical flakes of bread laid neatly in a row
The black of the table showing through their whiteness.

He takes one
The tongs gripping only its thin grey rind,
A nigh-imperceptible sag at its centre
Its wafery thinness bending as he lifts it through the air.

The stillness of the flame a single star
The bread as his body
The toasting as a necessary hardiness
A visible resilience.

He employs a complicated lateral motion
A spiral, a zigzag, a crosshatch, a path
Of his own unconscious devising ensuring
No single part of the bread will be heated
More than any other single part.

An unblemished toasting, the whiteness
Uniformly turned to black,
Stopping just before the bread catches fire
And burns to ash.

The few surviving slices
Laid out once again
To harden, to cool
He studies them
Assessing their merits
The thoroughness of their black.

And, certain the bread has been rendered inedible,
He gathers the slices and posts them
One by one out into space.

Then, Again

When their snuffling robotics discovered the whole planet empty
With not one squiggle of life to be found
But nonetheless gulped down
Small sterile packets of gas and grit
To bring the long way back for analysis

And though they had no need for such a place
Still they engineered new strains of plant life
That might yet thrive in that wasteland
But kept each pristine seed secure
From being released on home turf
Where soils and skies were simply far too rich

And when some seeds of course were smuggled out
And secretly released
And went completely haywire
Turning the whole world toxic just like that
So that the wind stopped working
And the mountains malfunctioned
And the seas settled into a singular heaviness
And all breathing things were suddenly uncoupled
From the tenuous chains that had for so long
Connected them to life

Those responsible turned their attentions
Back to the desolate planet
And took great comfort in knowing
They had alternative measures already in place.

Operational Guidance

He found her recharging herself in the sunroom
A low-ceiled circular space
One wide dome-window set into its roof

(There's no call to be heavy-handed
She'll think that she deserves it
She'll even seek out further punishment)

He had to crawl to get in
He wore deep amber goggles
He took shelter beneath a shady lip
That overhung the curved edge of the room

(And if you raise your voice against her
She'll only work harder
She'll burn out her coils
Straining in her utmost effort to please)

Laid full-length beneath the glass her whiteness
Stark against the black-tiled floor and glowing
With the brightness of the naked sun

(If you're in any way vague in your orders
Her actions will be no less resolute
She doesn't do things by half-measures)

The overlapping leaves of her irises
Stopped down to an aperture one micron in diameter
Still the starfield's pinholed light came through
Its speckle imprinted dimly
Onto the gilded sheen of wafered retinas

(If you make an offer to serve her
She'll not appreciate the irony
She'll act out a pretence
Of not having heard what you said)

When first he unpacked her
He found a faux-gold locket on a chain around her neck
Inside—a folded sheet of greaseproof paper
A finely printed list of usage notes

(If you choose to treat her gently she
Won't notice that anything's different
She'll never think that you might be at fault)

No wiring schematics
No buttons, no master switch
No way for him to fix her if she broke

(Any unreasonableness on your part
Will be matched by her complete subservience
She's foolproof, there being
No manner in which she can fail)

He squirmed beneath his ledge
She did not move

His sweat dripped sizzling onto the tiled floor
Her skin remained perfectly cool

He shuffled out the same way he came in
She went on recharging

Frequently Asked Questions

Now death can be postponed and birth prescribed
   to them that ask, what proportion of funding
   has been set aside for the hungry?
We've deconstructed matter to its darkest particles.
   The loops of our magnetic tunnels now run
   beneath five continents.

Have you swapped out the isotope scrubbers?
   Are the shoreline plastics waiting piously
   for their sublime incineration?
We've mapped out the stars to a depth of one third
   of the universe. We've ridden the gravity-quakes.
   We've noted how dingy it's getting.

The fish are gummed up with humectant.
   The crabs carry sandcastle shells.
   How long till the oceans are empty of all but their water?
We've unravelled the cryptogenera
   for all living things. We know the eye colour
   of prehistoric lice.

Can the purifications be trusted? Does a purge
   remove every last trace? Are there cracks in the brickwork
   through which the corrosion might seep?
We've found a new fuel source more potent than any before.
   We're splitting foundational strata
   to get the stuff out.

Beechwoods, bacteria, lichen, crows, stray dogs.
   Could we not focus more on the reanimation
   of all those we were forced to leave outside?
We've perfected our nigh-indestructible glassware.
   Not even a one-hundred-megaton blast
   could impair it.

Have you put all your boosters and shuttles away?
   Have you learned yet how to bring down
   all the junk you threw up?
We've jettisoned so much metal in close orbit
   you can see its magnificent sky-smear glinting
   on clear blue midsummer days.

Cooped up beneath the burden of a broken atmosphere
   is there reason enough to be found
   for our carrying on?
We've done all the groundwork.
   There's no price for progress.
   The new world is already prepped.

The Martian Ages

I

With one hand gripping the steering column
The other poised over the button for the brakes
He gazed fixedly through the windscreen

At the stars that no longer went wheeling
At the fine blue dot growing never any larger

And little black hairs began sprouting all over his skin
The hairs clumped together they melted
They formed a rough black shell
Encasing him completely.

His pale companion picked him smooth again.

II

With one hand dangling a brown beer bottle
The other loosely supporting a long black revolver
He sat out on his porch unrocking in his rocking-chair

Where the prairie grasses had no wind to sway them
Where the fly-screen's mesh was clogged with yellow dust

And his skin began to wrinkle
The wrinkles too began to wrinkle
Turning in then further in upon themselves
Enfolding him completely.

His pale companion ironed his creases out.

III

With one hand scooping up blue brackish water
The other fastened round a mangrove root
He hesitated at the slippery lip of the pool

In which his dark reflection was utterly still
In which his reflection stared into the night sky forever

And his black flesh started to harden
It crumbled and slid down into the water
Where his likeness received it without sentiment
Dissolving him completely.

His pale companion didn't see a thing.

Common Aspirations

As a peasant boy he looked for truth
In each fine granule of soil
And in deep irrigation ditches
And in the veins of black-leaved vegetation,
But he was too ignorant not understanding its voice.

And there were those who made the world to be this way,
And those who discovered it just the way it was.

(And every few years or so   a revelation)

As a runner-of-errands he knew truth resided
Hidden in sealed documents
And in the dregs of unwashed coffee cups
And at the ends of endless corridors,
But he'd not a moment to linger nor take stock.

And there were those who spoke out freely never doubting,
And those who kept things close unsure of the source.

(And every few years or so   an admitted mistake)

As a shipwright he glimpsed aspects of the truth
Riveted tightly between plate metal
And distilled into fuel from great napiform vats
And sparking bright between electrical connectors,
But he'd been relied upon never to mention such things.

And there were those who could hark right back to creation,
And those who ventured no further than what was recorded.

(And every few years or so   a medical breakthrough)

As the top rule-maker he hoped that truth lay curled
In decrees written out in his own fine hand
Or in the purity of as yet untested equations
Or in the always looming deeps of space,
But the void gave nothing back and the stars just blinked.

And there were those who implored him daily for the answer,
And those who thought him wise to have stayed quiet.

(And every few years or so   up went a rocket)

Of the Urge to Return

Like the tentative step towards
The seemingly fizzled fuse of a huge red firecracker
And the hand reaching out once again
With the end of the drooping taper fiercely glowing

Or the sponge cake far too long left in the oven
And still when the skewer is pushed in deep
Then slowly drawn back out
Its surface is inexplicably sticky with dough—

So there was always that nagging doubt
A persistent gnawing restlessness
The itch they knew it was probably best not to pester
That something they desperately needed had been left behind

And if they ever found it wasn't there
If absence yawned its heavy emptiness they also knew
They'd have to go on looking a little while longer
Just in case their methods had been wrong.

The Martian Makes Land

They'd spent all afternoon in search of accommodation,
A cabin in the mountains
A glorified beach hut
A misty white-walled cottage on the moors.
So many features for them to fuss over
So many vacancies.
He'd hover, she'd nip in
To check on general upkeep,
On the air-filtration system
On the state of hermetic seals.

They settled at a small riverside hotel
Their vehicle taking up most of the car park,
The road, the field behind it.
He felt sluggish
Tired and grouchy from the trip
He took slow heavy steps to the hotel's front door
While she zipped back and forth with their luggage.
And as she unpacked
He slumped himself into a chair by the window
Overlooking a lake that stretched to the horizon
Its deep blue waters mixing with
The deepening blue sky.

When the moon rose he squinted, blinked, it was
Uncomfortably bright.
Still he waited watching to find out
What other moon might eventually follow the first
To see which he preferred.
But when after hours no other moon showed
He grumbled and dragged his dead weight off to bed,
Feeling it was all a waste of effort
Feeling cheated.

The Hopes of the Martian Settlers

In hankering after meat, they made for themselves
A fungal mould—it being
As good a place as any to begin.
They dug a great pit and poured their new soup in.
It sloshed and settled filling the space it was given.

They'd perfected a foodstuff of vegetable blood
Strong black sap with a mineral bite
Along with this they tossed in every other chemical
Requisite to their existence.

They hoped someday for something planktonic
For nematodes, flatworms
For even the smallest of snails.

The mould took all they gave it, greedily
And with it made more mould.

In winter with thermal jackets they warmed it
Keeping it smooth-skinned and supple.
In summer they set up a sprinkler system
To hold its crust from cracking in the heat.

They hoped for cuttlefish, for jumbo shrimp
For horseshoe crabs, for trilobites
For maybe one plump little beetle.

But when the mould gave of itself only mould
They fed down cables and shocked it in its depths.
And when the only word it pronounced was mould
They bombarded it with free radicals.
They dropped in toxins, opiates, recyclables, waste.
They irradiated it.

They'd hoped for rainbow trout
For strawberry poison frogs
For snapping turtle, limbless skink
They'd hoped someday for a clutch of broiler hens.

And though the mould preferred to stay simply mould
It took to squirming up the sides of its enclosure.
It had a hankering to get away for a while
To spread itself further afield.

In a slow bid for freedom it pushed inwardly
To grow up
With baby steps oozed out—
Over the lip of the pit.

But when they saw it emerging
And when they saw it was no less mould
For all their careful encouragements
They took a blowtorch to it
And blasted every last jellied globule
Down into powdery ashes
And then, just to be certain
Blasted the ashes too.

After which they dug a new and bigger pit
And began the whole strained process over again.

Kindred

He wanted to begin his survey work.
She wanted to head into town.

A long march of billboards lined the city road
Every one a giant grinning face of welcome.
The martian piloted straight through the middle of each
Leaving a tunnel of gaping rag-edged holes.

In the square a lonely inhabitant
Having missed the last flight out
Had long ago turned to stone
Right in the act of heading for higher ground.
Too heavily set on its plinth to push over
The martian covered its head with a traffic cone
Not liking the manner in which it stared off into space.

In shop windows ranks of abandoned companions
Stood gazing through the glass for their maker's return,
Each one identically shaped
Though none was quite as white as the martian's own
As now she stalked through the aisles seeking matching apparel
Attempting to fit in.

And while she was changing the martian took
To battering the helpless figurines,
Popping out their hollow limbs
Skittering heads and torsos all about him.

Having left them suitably scattered,
A flop of empty sleeves and staring acquiescent eyes,
He felt more centred
He felt relieved.

His own companion returning
In a gingham shirt and washed-out dungarees
Untucking the tips of an auburn wig from her collar
Picked her way through the bloodless slaughter
With neither a smile nor a frown,
Both being beyond her.

She took the martian's upheld hand in hers
And allowed herself to be led outside
Without reservation
Without once looking down.

On a Tour of the Martian Caves

If the pale slender figures scratched onto the walls
Were said to reflect the first of intelligent life
It was only due to the sticks of white chalk being used
Standing out better against the slick black stone

And where these primitive artworks had been patterned
Out of smeary fingerprints
It was such as children
With small grubby hands often made

And if over countless generations
This record had been preserved though lightlessness
It was only because none but the bored and the work-shy
Ever ventured to loiter down this way

And if stopping to listen you thought you could hear
Their long-dead voices still murmuring through the caverns
The trick worked best if you spoke fairly loudly and clearly
Before shutting up

Clues

The martian began his work in search of any living thing.
He lifted and looked under warm wet stones
A well-known if perfunctory hiding place
But found no telltale holes in the crystalline soil.
He dropped the rocks and left them where they fell.

He collected up jam jars of water from guttering
Following heavy storms. He checked for tadpoles, algae, spawn,
For glass eels cycloned into cloud then redistributed here.
The samples under testing proved utterly clear.
He drank them down.

Descending in his diving bell to rest on the breathless
Ocean bed, beside a small dark pool that led
Still deeper, he sniffed at superheated vents but detected
Only a mineral purity. Sulphur hydride, silicates, salt-iron,
Smoke. He tugged twice on the rope to come back up.

He scoured through libraries for mites
That chewed on the glue of old spines but found
No more than signs of foxing,
Pencilled annotations, rubber-stamped overdue dates.
He muddled up the volumes on each shelf.

Heading home he strolled past warehouses,
School gymnasiums, churches, village halls.
He felt watched, that under each roof some huge
Monstrosity resided, peering out. He walked on smartly.
Not waiting. Not daring to look.

A Compromise

When the old rocket slumped to its knees
Amid the breakers in the bruise-black sands of the bay
The gathered martians gazed at it dumbly
Rubbing their leathery heads.
The mystery vessel had not been expected.

The passengers, packed in foam and sickly pale
Like tinned fish squashed up head to toe
Had made of themselves
A flimsy bloodless cargo.

They came seeking solace, a refuge, a future.
They promised not to take up too much room
Needing but a few spare roots to chew on.

But this was by no means the issue at hand
Where food grew thick and unclaimed land
Was always plentiful.
It was the stragglers' comparative old-world pallor
That caused consternation
A worry that such feebleness might spread.

The debate over what might be done lasted several weeks,
The vagrants all the while kept waiting, huddled on the beach.

At length, a decision—
The men were tied off
The women sewn up

                    And that
Seemed in some way to settle the matter.
Such measured mixless integration was acceptable.
Each incomer granted nothing less
Nor more than their natural span of days,
To which all living things are duly entitled.

The Martian Commutes

The routine of his breakfast bright
With early morning's glassy light,
He'd sip his tea, she'd zip him
Into his plasticated suit, test its robustness with
A small sharp pat on the back
Before passing him his battered briefcase
In which his sample jars and airtight lunchbox
Had been packed.

Across the hall from the martian's penthouse suite
His private elevator shaft,
The sudden start of that long descent
Lifting the weight for a moment from his feet.

The next floor on his list was deep underground.
He needed a secret code just to open the doors.
An automated hiss and purge
The chime of strip lights blinking on and there
Was the cold grey tunnel that led to the lab.

He stepped out. He stopped.
He considered his options.

She wouldn't show any surprise at his early return.
She'd have no concept of how long he'd been gone.
He'd get on with his jigsaw and she'd stand by
Ironing his cotton handkerchiefs.

He took a short step back and pressed
The button for the topmost floor.
The doors sucked slowly shut. The cables jerked.
He took the day off.

Ancient Trickery

The trick with the air was to capture a part of it
Inside a large soap bubble
And while the bubble maintained its wobbled integrity
Scramble the air it held till that air
Had turned into something quite other than air
And couldn't turn back
Finding strength and stability in its new structure
So that when at length the soap-skin split
And the un-air mixed with the old air it now touched
A word was passed
And a similar change was effected

The trick with the earth was to place a tight black ball of it
Under one of three small silver cups
Each of them identical so that it didn't matter
How fast they were shushed across the table-top
Nor in which order the cups were upturned
For what was revealed would no longer be
A tight black ball of earth but a tight black ball
Of something else entirely
Having lost all earthiness
And that whatever might then be done to that ball
It could not be made earthy again

The trick with the flesh required neither stooge nor assistant
It was open to everyone
And every sealed box was mirrorless
And each time the blades went in the cut was clean
And when the flesh was put back together
Those parts left behind were easily forgotten
So that with practice what the flesh became best at
Was its own daily performance
Remembering nothing of its former condition
With one self given up in gaining another

The mind watched all this very carefully
So as not to be fooled
And the mind knew when the soap bubble burst
The soap itself had not been tampered with
And the mind knew as it stared at the shushing cups
That each was made of the finest materials
And the mind knew as the flesh all around it closed in
That nothing underhand was going on
That here the truth was undeniable
So the mind all the while kept its eyes wide open
And followed on dutifully

The Martian Goes Hunting

Sneaking up in silence on a kitchen cabinet
The martian slid open a drawer
Plunged in his hand
And snatched up
A tin-opener

At once he tossed it back unwanted, useless
All the tins he'd found were aeons past their best-before

In the shadow of a sofa
He lurked
Choosing his moment before pouncing out
Upon a telephone

But he lunged clumsily and the telephone tumbled
Clattering to the parquet floor
Shattering its bakelite shell and spilling
Its stuffing of wires and primitive circuit boards

The martian wasn't bothered
In any case—such items were better off captured in pairs

Roaming deserted streets with his net held high
He encountered a host of discarded umbrellas
Slouching in doorways or flopped in the gutter
Or hanging upside down from electrical cables
Their torn silks flapping weakly in the wind

All of them broken
And he took no pleasure
In bagging something quite so handicapped

He turned on his heel

At home with his feet up in front of the fire
He was just nodding off when he spied
A wrought-iron poker

Faultless
Sleek
A perfect specimen

In form just as it had been for thousands of years

An exemplary survivor
A true original

Slowly he reached out
And took it
And had it
Its cool heavy droop in his hand
Ever eager for use

A worthy trophy for the long trip home

Of Martian Lovemaking

She arrived at the appointed late hour
A cautious advance through unlit gardens
To knock at his night-quiet house.
He was wary of what went hidden in the dark
He bustled her inside
Bolting the back door behind her.
She presented her official documents
A freshly laminated permit
A worn card folder containing her medical notes.
He took an age going through all the papers
Studying each for signs of forgery
For sly concealed clauses.

She set out bowls of refreshments.
He donned a pair of thin black rubber gloves.
She cracked the seal of herself and opened up
A packet of antiseptic wipes.
He closed his eyes to concentrate
Exerting an internal musculature
To tease himself out by raw pink increments.

She arranged herself comfortably
Over one arm of the sofa.
He fed himself bit by bit into the appropriate aperture
Consulting a pamphlet for guidance all the way in.
She squirmed
Hoping to angle herself more conducively
To his halting progress.
He jiggled till he felt a small part
Of what he presumed was still him
Inflating somewhere deep inside her.
She winced and reached forward for a magazine.
He counted dark spots on the ceiling to stop himself
Reading over her shoulder.

She jerked an arm round behind her
To get at an itch.
He reeled and almost snapped his baculum.
She went quiet
Resting her head on folded arms.
He wanted to pick at a small grey scab on her back
His free hand hovering inches above her
Before clenching into a fist and drawing away.

She felt something give
Releasing a tension she hadn't known was there
An unexpected hollow ache.
He found himself suddenly weightless
Slipping back
He staggered a bit before catching his step.

She bolstered the base of her spine with old cushions
Her short black legs raised stiff against the wall.
He hid himself in his room
With the sheets drawn high and all lights off.
And when she later knocked and when
She came in uninvited
He didn't move.
And when she stole right into bed beside him
He was forced to spend every hour of the night
Pretending to be asleep.

The Martian Visits the Museum

With hardly a glance the martian passed on
Through the well-trodden halls of industrial science
Devotional monuments to a numerical god
Such an obsession with heavy metals
A cumbersome religiosity.
He dragged his feet down corridors of warring paraphernalia
Each tiresome avenue showing
Ever more complicated ways in which to do
Something altogether straightforward.
But he lingered at the taxidermy cabinets
Marvelling at the balding scalps, the sunken cheeks
The joints reinforced with plaster and gauze
The dry and lustreless furs.

Leaning in he read each small blue plastic plaque
A common name above an etched extinction date.
He opened up the enclosures and set to work.

When he was finished
Several stiff-limbed impala were tangled
Through the wheels of a steam locomotive
While small varnished fish lay on their sides
Spaced evenly along the buffered tracks.
Above this numerous sun-dried insects
Their pins still sticking out
Had been glued to the green and yellow underside
Of a nine-foot gravity bomb.

A reticulated python had the barrel of a Lewis gun
Half-lodged down its gullet
The tip of its tail curled round and posted
Through the trigger guard.

Mismatched farm animals gleefully lowered each other
Into a nuclear reactor
Their trotters and teats glowing red.
A goggle-eyed Kodiak bear
Its hair on end its forepaws held aloft
Sat in the seat of the first lunar rover
Teetering on the brink of a high balcony.
While in the museum's central atrium
A resin-skinned sperm whale held in its prised-wide jaws
A kidney dialysis machine
Hard rubber hoses and bare-ended wires
Trailing from its teeth.

Heading on out past the front desk the martian
Reached up and tore off a season ticket.
There was still a great deal of work to be done
And he was sure to discover more stock in the museum's vaults.
He'd come back in a month or so to see
How things were progressing.

A Calculatory Flaw

And in the middle of counting up stars
All over again
When they realised their own existence wasn't
Merely a matter of quantity and
That they shouldn't weigh the numbers all at once
Making of their home one buzzing oddity
Among so much sterile space
But that each potential planetary residence must be considered
On its own individual merits
With a million specific parameters to be passed
For just one microbial speck to not only be formed
But to be content to be sustainable
With such a condition here just so
And others this way round and by no means that—
And in having assessed every distant planet they could discern
And finding that each failed in some fundamental way
So they turned their measurements inward
Viewing their own small strip of land
With the same dispassionate logical scrutiny
Only to discover it too failed on similar grounds
Of gross incredulity
That the likelihood of their own complication of living
Was just too dubious to be conceivable—
In an instant of mutual enlightenment
They chose to mark this revelation down
As anomalous
Such results were to be expected once in a while
And could be disregarded
As they made a slight adjustment to the initial parameters
And set about running their tests
All over again

Supplemental Matter

She'd been reading the same book for weeks.
It wasn't long and she didn't read quickly
The space for her to make new memories was limited
Was soon used up
So each time she got to the end of the last page
She began the book afresh.

One day he took it from her
She didn't protest.
He leafed briefly through it then taking a craft knife
He sliced out several pages
And passed it back.

She didn't mind the gaps
She couldn't see what wasn't there.
The mystery of what any full page implied
Had not been diminished by others being gone.

Again he took the book.
He cut out strips from each remaining page
Leaving the paragraphs topped and tailed
A lattice fixed within a marginal frame.

She found these word-strips easier.
She ran her fingers down their ladders
Followed along their rungs
Discovered patterns in their squirmy flow
Fresh meaning in their disconnectedness.

He cut into the individual words.
She waited, looming over him
Her eyes locked on the path the blade-tip took.
He left fragmented strings of letters
Isolated punctuation marks.

She accepted her book with both hands, tenderly.
She touched on the lacework of papers held
Secure between hard covers.
She studied the blacknesses
The angles and curves of each glyph
Their different sounds, their different silences.
She knew there was a code to be unravelled.
She let each shape seep in and do its work.

He went out, leaving her reading
Broke into a bookstore and searched along the shelves
For a pristine copy.
Returning he asked for her book one final time—
She gave it over readily.

Despite the strength of her attentiveness
She didn't see him make the switch.
She didn't notice anything had changed.
With what he gave back of just as much interest
As what he had taken away.

Round Dance

There was an old martian who lived all alone

He never cleaned his house nor tidied up
His bedsheets went unchanged
The walls were damp
And when his black skin flaked
As all skin does
It settled on the surfaces like soot

He had few visitors
He didn't mind
He found the smell the wetness comforting

A mould grew on the sooty dust and spread
It crept onto his sheets then onto him
It got under his fingernails
His skin
It got behind his eyes and peered out

Now visitors would find a brighter house
A freshness in his glance a spark a warmth

But those who choose to give are hard to please
And soon the mould had eaten him right through
His apathy his loneliness his use
All he'd received
Amenably removed

One spot of mould retreated from his shell
It sank into the walls
The house was sold

There was an old martian living all alone

Vitae Veritum

Following close to his hastily scribbled map
The martian came to the abandoned university.
Gaining admittance was easy
He had the requisite experience.

Lying safe within their hardy coats
Within separate resealable pouches
Within an airtight tin
Within a locked desk drawer
Within the principal's oak-panelled office
Were the first of the seeds, the prototypes
From which all martian cultivars were grown.

He shook the tin beside his ear
Then took it outside to the sandy quadrangle
Under the hard white light of the midday sun.

A hand-printed label was glued to each packet
He checked the ancient names against his list—
The marrowfat peas the black lentils the mung beans
The groundnuts the rices the hemp.

Heaping them all in his rubber-gloved palm
He watched as each seed crackled and fizzed and shivered
As they slowly crystallized.

He took one large yellow grain between thumb and forefinger
And squeezed it.
It burst into glittery dust.

The others he tipped and let fall to the flagstones
Leaving them scattered
A uniform dispersal.
Much better that way for everyone concerned.

Continuity Rites

I

When the pollen blew in as a heavy grey mist
It poured down over the cliffs to slop
Into the valley's cup.

At the head of the swamplands they waited
Their flat feet planted deep in boggy ground.

And the pollen stuck.
It glued their eyes shut, thick with mucilage
A gloopy coat, a wetness
That their warmth soon turned opaque.

And the pollen hardened round them
It formed a milky crust
Leaving them firmly rooted in the loam.

II

When the pollen blew in as a storm of red hailstones
It funnelled tight between the valley walls.

In warm shallow streams they stood ready.
In stagnant blue pools they held fast.

And the pollen blasted them naked.

It scoured them, digging its hard red grains
Through skin and flesh to leave them raw
To leave them cleansed, refreshed, still standing
Where waters carried pinkish foams downstream.

III

When the pollen blew in as a thick black smoke
It came with a violent wind to drive it forward.

They met it out on stony ground
And when it touched them it clung.
It made of them small rounded statues
A gritty blackness built up layer on layer.

The storm of pollen blew still more fiercely
Eroding the new figurines
Each of them steadily sharpened and thinned till
As black blades of stone
They toppled and crumbled away

Leaving no trace of them
Leaving the whole valley smooth.

The Trail Goes Cold

Standing at the border of a neatly furrowed field
The martian spied footprints on the ridges of soft black soil.
He knelt to examine one keen-edged impression
How the fine crystals of earth still held their shape.

He eased his own boot into it—a snug fit.
Perhaps he hadn't been the only one
Sent back all this way.
The others might still be ahead.

He followed the footprints from ridge to ridge
Till he reached the skeletal remains of a hawthorn hedge
And found the tracks ran on right through.
He stooped low and crawled in.

Soon it was so dark, so icy, so utterly airless inside
He couldn't move for fear
The unseen thorns all about him may, at any moment,
Snag upon and rip his suit. He lay very still.

  (She placed the pale back of her hand
  Against his cheek.
  She gave him broth to sip
  She steadied the spoon.
  She laid a cool wet flannel
  Over his troubled brow.)

He stood on the lip of a pebbly desert
That fell and rose in waves of sharp black stone.
The pebbles shifted and clacked as panting he slid
Down one side to scramble at once up the other.

There was now no sign of the footprints only
Deep depressions cresting each slope of stones.
His vision was misty with sweat. He couldn't tell
How many waves there were to go.

He was faint from exhaustion when after an age
He entered the eaves of a petrified forest
Its thick crooked boughs in a tangle above him
Shutting out the light.

   (She stripped him to the waist
   She helped him lie flat.
   She eased the shivers from him
   She smoothed out the aches.
   She rubbed warm butters of camphor and clove
   Into the tender creases of his skin.)

Before him was a slope of huge black boulders
Stacked to the height of mountains.
No possible way for him to climb over. He found
A dark partition in the foothills and squeezed himself through.

He was wading in water—a murky pool. Very soon
It was up to his neck, the water's thickness halting
Any further progress. He couldn't feel his own extremities.
He clung to a long fleshy root that brushed up against him.

   (She let him lie in the bath a while longer
   She added magnesium salts.
   She soaped him, she dried him
   She dressed him in cottons.
   She put him to bed with a hot-water bottle
   Watching while he slept.)

The Inheritance of a Martian Daughter

And when we showed her all the unworked lands
That would someday be hers
She dug a deep hole in the dank earth
And threw herself in

And when we pampered her with toys
With soft automatons
She lay on the floor of her room like a rag doll
With half her innards removed

And when we lavished her with beauty treatments
Of discreet epilation and purging herbal soaks
She pocketed a razor when we weren't looking
And bled herself out in the bath

And when we tried shock therapy
She pleaded that the voltage be increased
And when we made incisions in her temples
She gabbled on unceasingly urging us to scrape out ever more
    matter

And when at length we found her a willing partner
And handed her over
She thought she'd won and went away gladly
Till she discovered the nursery—its row of empty cribs

The Martian's Full Appraisal of the Situation

The low-spreading oak centring a field of wheat
Had turned to glass
Its leaves its branches all were glass

The wheat-stems were of yellow glass
They snapped and shattered falling as the martian
Trudged up slowly through the field

(if the ultimate purpose of his race
was its own prolonged survival
if mere existence was in itself a success
if existence on its own was everything)

The martian's companion sat perfectly still
Her back to the mill-wheel width
Of the oak tree's grey-glass trunk

For the companion to wait was like sleeping
And to sleep was akin to death it was
To be not present at all

(if there was neither right nor wrong to anything
where pure survival was concerned
if whatever he wanted of life was by dint of living
the only important aspect of his life)

Around the tree the green glass moss
Had turned to glass-dust
Where it had been trampled

An acorn dangling fell from its high branch
And landed between them both
A single heavy egg-smooth jewel

(if having been sent all this distance he
was in no manner beholden to those who had sent him
if in simply being himself he owed nothing
to any person other than himself)

For the companion there was no change no sense of flow
Only one long-drawn-out moment
It was all of a singular vitality

With his visor pressed to her chest the martian listened
To the soft whirr of her internal mechanics
To her central fluid pump

(if he might do whatever he might choose to do
if every action was for him exactly the right action
if without conscience there was no need
to worry and without worry no need to care)

Or was it just his own heart he could hear
A shrivelled hard black lump that stuttered
And knocked in the lightless cavity of his chest

(and if he thought he might never go back
if ever he felt he did not need to go)

Martian Lullaby

This cot was mine, its painted bars I gripped.
This tattered blanket I too soiled and sucked.
My milk in you, my parted flesh, my screams.
Someday you will be all that's left of me.

Your dress, the dress he lifted when we met.
Your folds, your vales, your softnesses, your scents.
Dark-eyed you'll draw him in, I'll guide you through.
Once more another me curled up in you.

To withered lips you'll raise the same small spoon.
My cracked and ragged skin you'll then put on.
Make wide the hole you dig, but not too deep.
My bones shall welcome yours, as now, to sleep.

Desecrations

Parking up at the cathedral green
Intrigued by the building's overblown artifice
Its frivolous granite brocade
Its twin spires aiming vaguely into space
The martian rapped at the door
But no one answered.
He pounded the wood and somewhere deep inside
The old cathedral pounded back
So in he went.

The first thing he saw was a stained-glass window
But finding too much variance in the light
To see other things clearly
He pitched a heavy bible
Hand-printed in blackletter script
With illustrated marginalia
As overcomplicated as the window
He now put it through
Letting the pure unfiltered sun shine in.

He tried a few notes of the organ
Then fistfuls
Then all manuals and pedals together
He tried different combinations of stops
But nothing he did made the noise
Seem any more pleasant, so
He took the altar linens and shredded them
Then tore the choir's garments into strips
Then cut rags of confessional velvet
And having suitably bunged up
Each of the organ's thousand or so pipes
He tried the keys again.
How easy it was to stifle such a shriek.

In the belfry he swung a huge hammer and struck
The biggest of the bells
A whacking great blow.
He was not in any way alarmed
By the long deep cry of the iron as it split
And no one came running.
The resounding vibrations brought no sustenance
They could not feed a family
Could not knock the enemy down.

At points around the upper balcony
Were perched colossal angels with wings outspread.
The martian pushed them off one after another.
In this the angels proved they lacked the passion
For unabashed self-preservation
Not one of them swerved from its rapid descent
Scattering chunks of marble among the pews.

Alone in a darkened corner a dry font stood.
The martian emptied three bottles of communion wine
Into its polished bowl but the wine
Was beyond being corked
Its gritty red sediment sank to the bottom
Leaving thick yellowish liquid above.
With a long black finger the martian swirled it
But it was no use no effort of his
Could make such juices flow as one again.

A painting of mother and child had been hung
In an alcove full of soft overlapping shadows.
Taking a small silver coin from the offertory box
The martian scratched away at the woman's face
In hope of whatever secrets lay beneath.

After a few waxy layers he reached bare cloth
Here he could descry faint pencil marks
A code that on its own held little worth.
He kept at it
Till at last he could put his hand
Right into the ragged hole he'd made in the canvas
To touch on the bare stone behind.
He groped for a while in the darkness.
The brickwork itself seemed solid enough
He decided to call it a day.

An effigy upraised in crucifixion
Caught the martian's eye as he was leaving.
He liked the look of this
He could feel the great weight of all that flesh
Pulling against the nails
The glossy stream of blood from the man's pierced brow
Was sticky in its stillness
It oozed eternally
The painted skin was cracked with pain
The mouth hung limply open in
An anguish of feeble defeat.

Here was something the martian could relate to.
Due punishment was always worthy
Of prominent display
A warning for others never to do
Whatever foolish thing this man had done.
Unhooking the whole sorry structure the martian
Shouldered both cross and man
And with a slow world-weary gait dragged them
Out of the dusty cathedral
To stow in the back of his car.

A Cautionary Tale

Three little martian boys got into
The neighbour's vegetable patch
One was choked by a snare as they scarpered
   His meats were minced into fertilizer
   His bones were ground up into meal

Two little martian boys got into
The neighbour's curing shed
One succumbed to the smoke and lay wheezing
   His shrivelled skin was cut into leathery thongs
   His small black teeth adorned the door as studs

One little martian boy got into
The neighbour's winter store
He was found with a trap clamped round his wrists
   His soft insides were stuffed out with straw
   A slender dowel was posted through his spine

———

Their pregnant mother some days later
Waddled over to apologise
Past fences lashed tight with rawhide and on
Down rows of flourishing crops to knock
At a door above which
A black doll had been hung
Lump-limbed and puffy-cheeked
Each eye socket plugged with a large white polished stone.

Sitting to a cup of camomile
The mother agreed
If it hadn't been perilous
It wouldn't have been an adventure and that

If they couldn't get by such simple obstructions
They weren't much suited to the present climate.

Heading home with one arm supporting a basket
Of groceries freshly uprooted
The other curled under the bulge of her belly
She took great care examining
The intricate locks affixed to every gate
Hoping her next-born child might have better luck
Hoping more so for a daughter.

The Well

It lay in the shady recess of a sandstone courtyard
A low curved wall of crude yellow brick marked out
Its sudden drop.
Trailings of ivy and pale bougainvillea
Brittled through exposure
Clung to its lips.
Beside this ever-open mouth a sign proposed
That it be fed with gold
And promised in return
Whatever gold alone could not procure.

From his vantage point upon the balcony the martian
Watched his companion carrying bullion
Earnestly across the yard
Taken from banks that no longer had need of it.
He saw her drop each gold bar in
He saw each sharp yellow gleam swallowed quickly by shadow
He heard no splash but noted
How she lingered
Gazing down into the gloom
Before she dashed away to fetch more gold.

When the bank's reserves were exhausted
She brought back monogrammed cufflinks, wedding rings,
Fob watches, cameo brooches, hatpins, teeth.
Little by little she carried them over
And dropped them in
And paused
Before continuing her search.

At length she resorted to scraping at leaf, at plating,
At electrical microcomponents
The flakes gathered up and pressed
Into a single golden pip.

This finely crushed foil so offered
Fell no differently
Than all she'd cast in before it
And still the cool well-waters rose no higher.
Nonetheless
She seemed satisfied
Returning to her duties with a lightness to her step the martian
Could not comprehend.

That night he was restless
He dreamed his companion
Stepped slowly backward into the well
And sank herself forever out of sight.
He dreamed that after she'd wished herself away
The water oozed up through the stones and overflowed
Then kept on rising, rising
Even to his room.

He woke and went down to the moonlit yard
And stood by the silent gape of the well
And stared hard into it.
In his hand a simple locket on its chain
He dangled it for a moment from his outstretched fingertips
Before letting it drop.
There was no splash
No sound at all
As though there was no water only cold black emptiness
As though his lonely scrap of gold fell for eternity.

And the martian in his relief slumped down
With his back to the well's low wall
In expectation
Of whatever the morning would bring.

The Reaches of Belief

Two martian children a boy and a girl
Lay side by side on a high white grassy plain
Beneath a dull yellow sky and the tight pink piercing dot
Of the ever-distant sun.

Here they argued lazily concerning their existence.

The boy believed the first of their race
Had wafted here on the back of a leaf-shaped asteroid
And if not that then they'd steered a fiery blue comet
And if not a comet a mineral moon
Had long ago been driven deep into the martian surface.

It might seem incredible but
If you waited a while
Such things were bound to happen eventually.

The girl believed it to be far less dramatic
And that long ago a certain native plant had fallen sick
And in straining its pods had pushed out
The first martian baby
A trembling soft black ball of flesh.

She believed too that all seeds had once been stones
That the martian weathers had slowly worked upon them
And some at length had become inexplicably fertile.

It might seem improbable but
Only a few were required to start things off
And sooner or later such numbers were bound to come up.

They argued still more wearily
Conceding at length to a third possibility

That the martians had long ago created themselves.
That out of an irrepressible urge to exist
The whole race had simply considered itself into being.

It seemed an unlikely proposal but
They were still merely children and hadn't yet learned
That no matter how hard
Or how many believed
Or who won the argument
Or whose grand theory was said to have been disproved
Or even if they believed in nothing at all
It made no difference to the actual truth.

However they had got here
Here they were.

But justifying whether or not to stay put
Was an argument both were far too tired to begin.

In Need of Refurbishment

By far its best feature, the real selling point
Was its walled garden
Vast and vaulted—
An ample enclosure.

But there was a problem.
The previous tenants in their hurry to get going
Had left all the lights on
And not just the lights
The generators were self-sustaining
In all those many years they'd never stopped.

So the rains in routine shifts continued falling
The wind machines kept turning
And the grasses, the bushes, the trees
All went on growing.
A gentle but persistent suicide.
As the tips of their roots pushed gradually through
The base of the brickwork and on into
The old reactive world beyond those walls—
So they let that outside sickness in.

But none of this was of much consequence.
What was vital
Was that it had good solid foundations
That it was built on sturdy ground.
All the softer stuff could be quite easily stripped out.

Of course it needed work, all places do
A bit of mortar here and there to patch up the holes
A few new panels for the sky
A little simple love and care.

New earth could be carted in from storage
And it was always possible to get one's hands
On quality seed, after which
From seeds to seedlings to saplings to dripping with fruit
Wouldn't take so very long.

The weather was convenient, reliable
Predictable.
Even the sun
If it dipped behind cloud
Would soon enough shine through again.

One could surely make a go of it
Somewhere to settle, somewhere to grow old.
And with such a head start
With patience
One might even be happy here.

The Body Martian

A pilgrimage for the rising of the winter solstice sun
Ended in a narrow gully tapering down to a cliff
A steep-sided funnel of smooth grey stone
Packed with martians all straining to get the best view
Till those impatient at the rear began as one to push
And those up ahead ceased all at once to be martian
Behaving instead like a fluid under force
As surges pressed them now unavoidably onward
And so with nowhere to go their bodies became
As one body squeezing and splitting and merging
Till only a treacle-like substance remained
Oozing down the cliff that tipped the gorge
Beneath the cool pink glare of the new-risen sun
The organisers had to charge more in subsequent years

II

Due to overcrowding at desirable locations
Where all manner of modern conveniences abounded
The martian town-planners were forced to build rapidly upward
A grand fabrication so tall it pierced the sky's protective films
Till some idler at ground level tossed
A cigar-stub into a bin and soon the whole edifice above was clad
In fierce white flame and clambering oily smoke
Where those still trapped inside ceased at once to be martian
Becoming merely fuel unseasoned and damp
That whined and hissed as juices were boiled and released
And one by one their small black bodies popped
Till all that remained were piles of smouldering ash
For others to gather for others to press into bricks
Ready to start the building work afresh

III

When new prospects were discovered far out
Across milky martian seas there was a race
To mine them for their costly minerals
But the first great ships returning were unbalanced
Their holds crammed with a press of heavy ore
And sitting low between monstrous white waves
They soon succumbed and in that sudden sinking
The jettisoned crews ceased all at once to be martian
The abandoned cargo of their bodies
Bobbing for a while till full of sea
Each of them became at one with water
The only evidence of their excursion being
A perfectly preserved logbook floating ashore
Through which an insurance claim was later lodged

Confessional

For years I worked at the observatory.
Each night I had my stint at telescopes both radio and optical
Twinned to the same sky-segment the one
To which I'd been assigned.
My very own column of space.

It went on almost to infinity
Tapering gradually outward, though
The circle of view down which I nightly stared
Remained quite small.

One distant slice of sky might house a billion billion stars
And then, just a little way further,
A billion times that many stars again
Etc.

The work was in essence straightforward—
We sent out our signals
They travelled forever
I listened for whatever might come back.
A pattern in the crackle
A nonrandom tone
An indistinct disturbance in the light.
I would have been content with anything.

Of course we'd been sending out broadcasts for years
Symphonies afternoon dramas the weather the news.
We couldn't stop such signals going up.

And when one evening the power went off
And I sat in the dark and the silence that really
Was not so very different from how it felt
When all the many machines were functioning,
In that break that moment that pause I realised

If life was truly out there
Somewhere
Either in my sky-tube or in another's
Then one thing was certain—
They didn't know we were here.

To have heard our signals they'd surely need
Receivers of their own and with such receivers
Their own internal broadcasts
Sent out accidentally
Just like ours.

But we'd never picked up a thing.
And if so we hadn't
Then neither had they.

Which could mean they didn't have radios, or
That there really was no one there, or that
The gap between our stars was still too great.

It didn't matter which
And when the power buzzed back on
My work resumed.

There always was more listening to be done.

Last Suppers

With each home-cooked meal they'd boxed up
And stowed in his hold
His superiors had added a note
Tucked into a flap on the lid,
Sealed and dated, matched to his rigid agenda.

When they said he should by now have the Earth
Full-blued in his telescope
He was looking the other way
He was making dot-to-dot patterns with the plentiful stars
Practically any shape was feasible
With a little effort.

When they said he should be at the first test location
He was lounging in the bows of a rowing boat
At the still centre of a lake
His pale companion in charge of the oars
As they headed steadily out over unplumbed depths
Towards a tiny tuft of land.

When he should have been loading up crates of sample jars
He was mending an old reflex camera
He had no rolls of film
He just liked the sound of the shutter
He liked to turn the lens till through the ground-glass viewfinder
All the competing lines of the world matched up.

When he should have been prepping the rocket for relaunch
Having filled up the tank
Having wiped down the windscreen
He was poking about an industrial complex
He was walking a wire between mile-high chimney stacks
He was pulling the plug of a dammed-up reservoir.

When he was due to be passing the boundary moons
He was teaching his companion
How to lay a brick
How to fold warm latex into cement
How to use not only the flat but the tip of the trowel
Spreading the glossed mix thick like molasses or malt.

When the swamplands should have been visible
When he should have been on hand for catchment
He was counting out chickpeas into containers
Putting some aside to replant
Others to soak
He was drawing up lists.

His lunchboxes were by now all empty
But they were of good quality, were washable, reusable
And with their lids off could be stacked together
Each one nestling snugly into the next.
In all they took up very little space.

Martian Mathematics

They decided to give simply everything a number—
They thought that this would mightily improve things
Such work might take a while but it would be worth it
All manner of things became plausible with numbers
Anything conceivable could be made out of a number.
To space at first they gave three numbers
Though these were flexible, negatable
To time they gave but one little seed of a number
An insignificant crumb sown a long way behind them
But it grew rapidly and soon caught up
Then sped on into the distance so far they couldn't see its end
And would have been wholly unmanageable
Except they only ever cut from it very thin slices
To put into service as and when required.
With such numbers they could do fantastic things
They clashed tiny numbers together at increasing speeds
To see what other numbers might fall out
They made fine incisions in one long number
Then fed in smaller numbers to writhe round inside it
And in this way made numbers that were extraordinary
Impossibly intricate clearly incredible numbers
Numbers the likes of which had never been seen.
And though they still hadn't found a sustainable method
By which to convert the new numbers they'd made
Back into something useful into something tangible
That didn't matter
With flawless adherence with stringent endeavour
They hoped yet to live out their dream of a world broken down
Into standardised modular units—
So much easier that way to bring things to order
So much easier to mould.

The Martian Stands Well Back

Not wanting to presume undue responsibility
For what he'd never felt was really his
He showed her the control panel
All its bright buttons and fancy dials

He showed her the labels he'd stuck underneath
With actions written large in simple words
And taking her cool white hands
He laid them limply in position

He unfolded large black maps for her
Plotting a pale curve of dashes through the dots
He watched her fingers trace the path he'd marked out

He lifted vital circuit boards from their slots
And prompted her to touch them hoping
She'd discover a natural affinity with such things

He left her detailed instructions in numbered steps
That she might follow with ease
Then squeezed her
Tight into a padded seat
Never meant for her to occupy

He bade her stay
He looked her hard in the eye
Then screwed the lower hatch shut as he left.

Watching from a safe distance
It was a while before he saw any movement
Till a tall white figure crept out and came all the way over
To stand right beside him
Looking up just as he looked

A little while longer and two of the turbines fired

There followed a palpable splutter
Amid a lot of thick blue smoke

The rocket first teetered on two legs
Then toppled over
Its nose buried deep in a splintering of woodland
Its hindmost strut raised stiffly into the air.

And though the martian never did know
Quite what his companion had done
He didn't much care
It wasn't his problem any more.

Soul, Searching

What came first—the soul
  or the soul's speckled egg?
Whatever creature laid that egg was but one step away
  from possessing the soul after which it had so yearned,
  but the soul devoured the mother once it hatched.

If unlimited numbers of undying souls were each given
  a typewriter, how long would it be till just one of them
  stumbled upon an original thought?
Only a single literate soul is required
  as well as a wish to apply itself to the problem,
  simpler souls will bash at the same small cluster of keys
  for an eternity growing never any wiser
  and even sturdy typewriters will break.

How can you tell if this is a soul half-full
  or a soul half-empty?
It depends upon what was poured into the soul
  and why it was so unfulfilling
  or upon who attempted to drain it and why they too
  so soon gave up.

If a soul cries out in loneliness is it surprised
  at its own lost voice?
To those who have ears to hear
  let them hear—
  but to those who have none
  let such pleadings reverberate deeply
  silently.